Clara Hughes

Terry Barber

WOMEN
WHO
INSPIRE

Clara Hughes is published by
Grass Roots Press, a division of Literacy Services of Canada Ltd.

www.grassrootsbooks.net

ACKNOWLEDGEMENTS

We acknowledge the financial support of the Government of Canada through the Canada Book Fund (CBF) for our publishing activities. Canadä

Produced with the assistance of
the Government of Alberta through the
Alberta Multimedia Development Fund. *Alberta*

Editor: Dr. Pat Campbell
Image research: Dr. Pat Campbell
Book design: Lara Minja

Library and Archives Canada Cataloguing in Publication

Barber, Terry, date, author
        Clara Hughes / Terry Barber.

(Women who inspire)

ISBN 978–1–926583–43–3

        1. Hughes, Clara. 2. Athletes—Canada—Biography.

3. Olympics—Participation, Canadian. 4. Readers for new literates. I. Title.

PE1126.N43B36323 2017   428.6'2   C2011–907702–7

Printed in Canada.

Contents

The athletes march in a parade.

Olympic Star

In 2010, Canada hosts the Winter Olympics. Canada is proud to be the host. Every Olympics opens with a parade. Athletes carry their country's flag in the parade. There's a secret in the air. Who will carry Canada's flag?

The host city for the Olympics is Vancouver.

Clara carries the flag.

Olympic Star

Clara Hughes carries Canada's flag. Clara enters the **stadium**. Her smile lights up the stadium. Clara waves Canada's flag. Canada's other athletes follow. They wave to the crowd. These athletes will win 26 medals for Canada.

Clara is a speed skater in the 2010 Winter Olympics.

Clara waves to the crowd.

Olympic Star

Clara wins a bronze medal in speed skating. The race is 5,000 metres. Clara hears her fans. Their cheers are loud. After the race, Clara turns to the crowd. She says: "Thank you. Once again you gave me wings."

Clara is 37 years old at the 2010 Olympics.

Clara trains for the 2010 Olympics.

Olympic Star

Clara fails to win the gold medal. But Clara does her best in the race. Clara believes that doing your best is important. Doing your best is more important than a medal. But Clara has not always done her best.

Clara's father likes to drink.

Early Years

Clara is born in 1972. Her father drinks too much. Her parents can't live together. Her father moves out. Clara and her older sister blame themselves. Like many teens, Clara finds trouble. Sports have no place in Clara's life. Trouble does.

Clara's parents separate when she is nine years old.

Teens smoke and drink at a party.

Early Years

Clara runs away from home. Clara smokes. Clara smokes a pack a day. Clara uses soft drugs. Clara drinks too much. Clara likes to party. Clara steals. Clara has no goals. Clara has no dreams. Trouble is Clara's best friend.

Clara grows up in Winnipeg, Manitoba.

Gaétan Boucher skates in the 1988 Olympics.

Early Years

Clara watches the 1988 Olympics on TV. She sees a speed skater. She loves how he moves. She loves how he **glides** on the ice. He looks so alive. Clara thinks, "That's what I'm going to do. That's what I'm going to be."

Gaétan Boucher is Clara's **role model**.

Clara's life changes direction.

Clara's Dream

Clara wants to be a speed skater. Clara wants to skate for Canada. Now, Clara has a goal. Now, Clara has a dream. Clara knows she can change her life. Clara is 16 years old.

Clara hangs up her skates.

Clara's Dream

Clara trains as a speed skater. In 1990, a cycling coach **recruits** Clara. She decides to hang up her skates and change sports. She works hard to become a cyclist. Clara rides in all sorts of weather. She trains to be her best.

Clara wears her bronze medal at the 1996 Olympics.

Clara's Dream

Clara's best is excellent. Clara becomes a world-class cyclist. She makes the Olympic team. In 1996, Clara cycles in the Summer Olympics. Clara wins two bronze medals. Clara is one of the best cyclists in the world.

This woman feels depressed.

Clara's Depression

Two bronze medals. Clara should be on top of the world. But Clara's medals are not gold. Clara feels no worth. She starts to eat too much. She starts to sleep too much. She cries too much. Clara is depressed.

Clara suffers from depression for two years.

Clara skates in the 2002 Olympics.

Clara's Depression

Clara's coach tells Clara she is fat and lazy. Clara makes a big decision. Clara fires her coach. A new coach enters Clara's life. Clara becomes a better cyclist. But she wants to skate again. Clara wants to skate in the 2002 Olympics.

Clara holds her bronze medal.

Clara Wins Gold

Once again, Clara trains as a skater.
She wants to make the Olympic speed
skating team. Clara trains for seven
months. Seven months is a short time
to train for an Olympic sport. Clara
makes the team. She skates in the
2002 Olympics.

Clara wins a
bronze medal in
speed skating
in 2002.

Clara shows joy after winning a gold medal.

Clara Wins Gold

Four years pass. Clara skates again in the 2006 Olympics. This time, she wins a gold and a silver medal. By 2010, Clara stands alone in Olympic history. She is the only person to win **multiple** medals in both the Summer and Winter Olympics.

Clara wins six Olympic medals.

Clara has a big heart.

Clara's Big Heart

Sports change Clara's life. Clara wants to give back. She wants to help children. Children who play sports tend to stay in school. Clara wants children to see the power of sports. She wants all children to have goals.

Children play with a ball made from rags.

Clara's Big Heart

Many children cannot afford balls or books. Clara donates money to a **charity**. She donates $10,000. The charity **promotes** sports. The charity also promotes education. The charity is called Right to Play.

Clara signs some **autographs** for children.

Clara's Big Heart

Right to Play helps children around the world. Clara travels to other countries to help Right to Play. Clara knows children need role models. Clara is a role model for others. She helps children reach their goals.

Clara also donates to a charity called Take a Hike.

Clara speaks about her depression.

Clara's Big Heart

Clara also helps people who suffer from depression. Clara becomes their voice. Clara talks about her weight gain. Clara talks about not wanting to train. Clara's voice helps others see that depression isn't shame.

One in five people have mental health issues.

Clara rides across Canada.

Clara's Big Heart

In 2013, Clara bikes across Canada. She stops in cities along the way. Clara talks to people about mental health. She talks about her depression. Clara wants others to share their stories. People do not feel alone when they share.

Clara bikes for 110 days.

Clara greets her fans.

Clara's Big Heart

To Clara, dark times make the good times even better. People respect Clara for her Olympic success. People also respect Clara's work to help others. Clara is a role model for youth. Clara is a role model for people with mental health issues.

Clara trains for the 2012 Olympics.

Clara's Big Heart

Clara competes in one more Olympics.
Clara cycles in the 2012 Olympics.
She is close to 40 years old. Clara fails
to win a medal, but she does her best.
Sports give Clara more than medals.
Sports give Clara the strength to help
others.

Glossary

autograph: the signature of a famous person.

charity: an organization that helps people in need.

glide: to move smoothly.

multiple: more than one, many.

promote: to support and encourage.

recruit: to find suitable people to join a team or company.

role model: a person whose behavior is copied by others.

stadium: a large open area with seats.

Talking About the Book

What challenges did Clara Hughes overcome?

Discuss why Clara is an athlete for all seasons.

Why does Clara stand alone in Olympic history?

Why is it important to talk about depression?

How does Clara "give back" to society?

Picture Credits